19/12/88

The peace of Christ

be with you today and always

Marion

Words of
PEACE

Copyright © 1978 Lion Publishing

Published by
Lion Publishing plc
Icknield Way, Tring, Herts, England
ISBN 0 85648 298 6
Albatross Books
PO Box 320, Sutherland, NSW 2232, Australia
ISBN 0 86760 209 0

First edition 1978, under the title *A Word of Peace*
Reprinted 1980, 1982, 1983, 1984 (twice), 1985

Photographs by Peter Baker, pages 9, 13,
37, 45; A.J. Deane, pages 35, 39; Tim
Dowley, page 17; Fritz Fankhauser, page 7; Lion
Publishing/David Alexander, pages 11, 15, 25,
29, 43; Phil Manning, pages 19, 31; Middle East
Archive, page 21; John Stedman, pages 23, 27,
33, 41

Quotations from *Good News Bible*, copyright 1966,
1971 and 1976 American Bible Society; published
by Bible Societies/Collins

Printed and bound in Hong Kong

Words of
PEACE

GOD GIVES PEACE

The Lord gives strength to his people
and blesses them with peace.

PSALM 29:11

GOD SETS THE TIME

Everything that happens in this world
happens at the time God chooses.
He sets the time for birth and the time for
death,
the time for planting and the time for
pulling up. . .
He sets the time for finding and the time for
losing,
the time for saving and the time for
throwing away,
the time for tearing and the time for
mending,
the time for silence and the time for talk.
He sets the time for love and the time for
hate,
the time for war and the time for peace.

ECCLESIASTES 3:1,2,6-8

PERFECT PEACE

You, Lord, give perfect peace
to those who keep their purpose firm
and put their trust in you.
Trust in the Lord for ever;
he will always protect us.

ISAIAH 26:3-4

'MY PROMISE'

'In the time of Noah
I promised never again to flood the earth.
Now I promise not to be angry with you
again;
I will not reprimand or punish you.
The mountains and hills may crumble,
but my love for you will never end;
I will keep for ever my promise of peace.'
So says the Lord who loves you.

ISAIAH 54:9-10

GOD'S CHILDREN

Happy are those who work for peace;
God will call them his children!

MATTHEW 5:9

AT PEACE

A child is born to us!
A son is given to us!
And he will be our ruler.
He will be called, 'Wonderful Counsellor,'
'Mighty God,' 'Eternal Father,'
'Prince of Peace.'
His royal power will continue to grow;
his kingdom will always be at peace.
He will rule as King David's successor,
basing his power on right and justice,
from now until the end of time.
The Lord Almighty is determined to do all
this.

ISAIAH 9:6-7

THE PATH OF PEACE

Our God is merciful and tender.
He will cause the bright dawn of salvation
to rise on us
and to shine from heaven on all those
who live in the dark shadow of death,
to guide our steps into the path of peace.

LUKE 1:78-79

'THERE WERE SHEPHERDS . . .'

There were some shepherds in that part of the country who were spending the night in the fields, taking care of their flocks. An angel of the Lord appeared to them, and the glory of the Lord shone over them. They were terribly afraid, but the angel said to them,
'Don't be afraid! I am here with good news for you, which will bring great joy to all the people. This very day in David's town your Saviour was born—Christ the Lord! And this is what will prove it to you; you will find a baby wrapped in strips of cloth and lying in a manger.'

Suddenly a great army of heaven's angels appeared with the angel, singing praises to God:
'Glory to God in the highest heaven,
and peace on earth
to those with whom he is pleased!'

LUKE 2:8-14

GOD PROMISES PEACE

I am listening to what the Lord God is
saying;
he promises peace to us, his own people,
if we do not go back to our foolish ways.
Surely he is ready to save those who
honour him,
and his saving presence will remain in
our land.
Love and faithfulness will meet;
righteousness and peace will embrace.

PSALM 85:8-10

BE BRAVE

Jesus said:
'Do you believe now? The time is coming,
and is already here, when all of you will be
scattered, each one to his own home, and I
will be left all alone. But I am not really
alone, because the Father is with me. I have
told you this so that you will have peace by
being united to me. The world will make
you suffer. But be brave! I have defeated the
world.'

JOHN 16:31-33

'MY OWN PEACE'

Jesus said:
'Peace is what I leave with you;
it is my own peace that I give you.
I do not give it as the world does.
Do not be worried and upset;
do not be afraid.
You have heard me say to you,
"I am leaving, but I will come back to you."'

JOHN 14:27-28

MAKING PEACE BY HIS DEATH

Christ himself has brought us peace by making Jews and Gentiles one people. With his own body he broke down the wall that separated them and kept them enemies.

He abolished the Jewish Law with its commandments and rules, in order to create out of the two races one new people in union with himself, in this way making peace. By his death on the cross Christ destroyed their enmity; by means of the cross he united both races into one body and brought them back to God.

So Christ came and preached the Good News of peace to all—to you Gentiles, who were far away from God, and to you Jews, who were near to him. It is through Christ that all of us, Jews and Gentiles, are able to come in the one Spirit into the presence of the Father.

EPHESIANS 2:14-18

'PEACE BE WITH YOU'

It was late that Sunday evening, and the disciples were gathered together behind locked doors, because they were afraid of the Jewish authorities. Then Jesus came and stood among them. 'Peace be with you,' he said.

After saying this, he showed them his hands and his side. The disciples were filled with joy at seeing the Lord.

Jesus said to them again, 'Peace be with you. As the Father sent me, so I send you.'

JOHN 20:19-21

THE FRUIT OF THE SPIRIT

The Spirit produces love, joy, peace, patience, kindness, goodness, faithfulness, humility, and self-control. There is no law against such things as these.

GALATIANS 5:22

LIFE AND PEACE

To be controlled by human nature results in death; to be controlled by the Spirit results in life and peace.

ROMANS 8:6

PEACE OF MIND

Don't worry about anything, but in all your prayers ask God for what you need, always asking him with a thankful heart. And God's peace, which is far beyond human understanding, will keep your hearts and minds safe in union with Christ Jesus.

In conclusion, my brothers, fill your minds with those things that are good and that deserve praise: things that are true, noble, right, pure, lovely, and honourable. Put into practice what you learnt and received from me, both from my words and from my actions. And the God who gives us peace will be with you.

PHILIPPIANS 4:6-9

'THE PEACE THAT CHRIST GIVES'

You are the people of God; he loved you and chose you for his own. So then, you must clothe yourselves with compassion, kindness, humility, gentleness, and patience. Be tolerant with one another and forgive one another whenever any of you has a complaint against someone else. You must forgive one another just as the Lord has forgiven you.

And to all these qualities add love, which binds all things together in perfect unity. The peace that Christ gives is to guide you in the decisions you make; for it is to this peace that God has called you together in the one body . . .

COLOSSIANS 3:12-15

FAITH AND PEACE

Now that we have been put right with God through faith, we have peace with God through our Lord Jesus Christ. He has brought us by faith into this experience of God's grace, in which we now live . . .

ROMANS 5:1-2

SEEDS PLANTED IN PEACE

Where there is jealousy and selfishness, there is also disorder and every kind of evil. But the wisdom from above is pure first of all; it is also peaceful, gentle, and friendly; it is full of compassion and produces a harvest of good deeds; it is free from prejudice and hypocrisy. And goodness is the harvest that is produced from the seeds the peacemakers plant in peace.

JAMES 3:16-18

THE GOD OF PEACE

May the God of peace provide you with every good thing you need in order to do his will, and may he, through Jesus Christ, do in us what pleases him. And to Christ be the glory for ever and ever! Amen.

HEBREWS 13:20-21